KEYBOARD INSTRUMENTS

JAMES YORKE

KEYBOARD INSTRUMENTS

AT THE VICTORIA AND ALBERT MUSEUM

V&A

Published by the Victoria and Albert Museum, London
First published in 1986

© Trustees of the Victoria and Albert Museum

ISBN 0 948107 04 9

Designed by Patrick Yapp
Typeset by Merrion Letters, London
Printed in Great Britain by Butler & Tanner Ltd.,
Frome and London

FRONT COVER: Harpsichord by Jean-Antoine Vaudry,
Paris, 1681.

BACK COVER: Spinet 'Queen Elizabeth's Virginals',
probably Venetian, c. 1570.

REVERSE OF COVER: A page from the Fitzwilliam
Virginal Book. Reproduced by Permission of the
Syndics of the Fitzwilliam Museum, Cambridge.

FRONTISPIECE/TITLE PAGE: Grand piano,
Robert Wornum & Sons, London, c. 1870.
Detail of the lid designed by John Gamble (1847-1911),
depicting Apollo and his lyre on one panel and a swan
on another, and detail of one side depicting the musical
instruments acquired by Carl Engel (1818-82) for the
Museum's collection.

Contents

Foreword

This picture book has been compiled by my colleague James Yorke who has also written the brief and concise introduction and historical survey which draws attention to some of the more important aspects of the Museum's fine collection of keyboard instruments.

Peter Thornton
Former Keeper
Department of Furniture and Woodwork
and of the National Collection of Musical Instruments
Victoria and Albert Museum
London, 1986

Introduction

The National Collection of Musical Instruments, which is housed at the Victoria and Albert Museum, is particularly renowned for its keyboard instruments. Even though this collection is by no means the largest in the world it can boast of keyboard instruments of great musicological importance, such as one of the earliest dated harpsichords, by Jerome of Bologna (1521), 'Queen Elizabeth's Virginals' and the Taskin miniature harpsichord.

The four main types of keyboard instruments – the harpsichord (with its variants, the spinet and the virginal), the clavichord, the organ and the piano – are represented in the collection, but that of the harpsichords and pianos is particularly strong. They range in date from the early sixteenth century to the early twentieth.

The nucleus of the collection was formed in the nineteenth century by Carl Engel, a distinguished musicologist, who not only published a great deal of original research on early music but also collected ancient instruments. Under his guidance, the South Kensington Museum, as the Victoria and Albert was then called, made many fine acquisitions, often at remarkably low prices, even by the standards of the period. Since his death in 1882 the collection has doubled in size, although during the present century purchases have been made mainly for their decorative qualities. In recent years, there has been a growing awareness of the musicological aspect, and certain keyboard instruments have been restored to playing condition. Measured drawings have also been made available for those who wish to make copies of them. A full catalogue of the keyboard collection, *Musical Instruments I : Keyboard* by Dr Howard Schott, has been published and a booklet on the decorative aspect of musical instruments, *Musical Instruments as Works of Art* by Peter Thornton, is also available.

Historical Survey

Representations of keyboard instruments are to be seen in medieval church carvings and illuminated manuscripts but the earliest representation which clearly shows octaves of eight naturals and five accidentals appears in the Ghent Altarpiece by Hugo and Jan Van Eyck (c. 1426), where St Cecilia is depicted playing a positive organ.

One of the earliest dated keyboard instruments, however, is a harpsichord of 1521 (1), built by Jerome of Bologna, a craftsman active in Rome in the early sixteenth century.

'Music when soft voices die' (1893) by Sir William Quiller Orchardson R.A. (1832-1910), depicting the upright 'Giraffe piano' by Van der Does, Amsterdam, c. 1820 (*colour plate* VIII). The instrument was presented to the Museum by the painter. Reproduced by courtsey of Courtauld Institute of Art.

The instrument probably had an original range of fifty notes and a single set of strings. The other great harpsichord of this century in the Victoria and Albert collection (5) was built by Giovanni Baffo, a Venetian, who worked to extraordinarily high standards of accuracy, though his instruments have undergone some unfortunate restorations in later times.

As well as the harpsichords, shaped rather like the modern grand piano, there are some fine Italian spinets of the sixteenth century in our collections. As with harpsichords, the sound is produced by a quill, at the top of a jack, which in turn is activated by a key: the quill plucks the string. The sixteenth-century spinet was usually hexagonal, and it was to a harpsichord what an upright piano is to a grand piano today. The most important examples of a spinet are 'Queen Elizabeth's Virginals' (which although called 'a pair of virginals' is a spinet, probably of Venetian origin), the jewelled spinet by Annibale dei Rossi (*colour plate* IV) and the Marco Iadra spinet (4), which has recently been restored to produce a fine, powerful sound.

Excellent instruments, with a high standard of craftsmanship, were made in Venice. They were often lavishly decorated, not only with gilding and painted arabesques but also with mythological scenes, such as Orpheus and the wild beasts, Apollo and the Muses, and Arion and the dolphin. By the end of the sixteenth century a second manual of keys was introduced in some instances. To begin with, music played on this keyboard was transposed down a fourth to make playing continuo easier. As the next century progressed, the two different manuals were used to activate different registers of strings, or stops (to use the correct term), thus emphasizing different tones.

Widespread in Europe was the claviorganum, a combination of harpsichord (or spinet) and organ: a second spinet by Annibale dei Rossi (3) in the collection has been used in such a combination. The only surviving English keyboard instrument of this century is a claviorganum (6 and 7) built by Lodewyk Theewes in 1579, a Flemish craftsman then working in Southwark. In fact, no other English keyboard instrument survives between that date and 1622, when John Haward built the Knole Park harpsichord.

By the beginning of the seventeenth century, Antwerp had become the centre of harpsichord making in Northern Europe, with the finest examples being made by the Ruckers family. Their instruments were renowned for the quality of their sound. In the Victoria and Albert Museum, there are two genuine Ruckers instruments, one made by Andreas Ruckers the Elder (9), and the other by Ioannes Ruckers the Younger (10); both were enlarged in the eighteenth century to accommodate the demands of contemporary music. Indeed, Ruckers harpsichords remained in demand well into the eighteenth century and, when the genuine article was unobtainable, imitations were made, disguised with Ruckers-type decoration and a plausible date. One such instrument (15), dated '1634', is at Ham House; it is thought to have been made about 1730.

There are two English virginals of this century in the Victoria and Albert Museum collection, one by Thomas White (11) and the other by John Loosemore (12). They are both rectangular in plan but their sound and playing mechanisms are essentially those of the spinet. Their sound is powerful and bright but their decoration is crude. During the second half of the seventeenth century, such instruments fell from favour and their place was taken by wing-shaped spinets, like that by John Player (13) which has a stand of turned wood.

In the eighteenth century, the finest harpsichords were made in France and England. One can see this development beginning in the seventeenth century, with such works as the 1681 Vaudry harpsichord (*colour plate* VI), an instrument with a fine, clear tone, exquisitely decorated with chinoiserie-cum-pastoral motifs. Vaudry was appointed instrument maker to Louis XIV. The French harpsichord builders extended the bass to FF, chromatically, to meet the demands of composers of the time, like Couperin and Rameau. The outstanding makers in Paris were the Goermans and the Blanchet families. Pascal Taskin, perhaps the greatest of the eighteenth-century makers, married into the Blanchet family. An example of Taskin's work is in the Victoria and Albert Museum (*colour plate* VII): it is a harpsichord with a keyboard of a very narrow compass, presumably for a child. It has been suggested that it was made for the Duchesse de Choiseul, an exceptionally small woman, who had special furniture made for her. She played the harpsichord accompanied by the Duc, on the flute. It has a beautifully decorated case and must have been very expensive.

It was during the eighteenth century that English harpsichords became renowned throughout Europe, and this was largely brought about by Jacob Kirckman and Burkat Shudi, immigrants from Germany and Switzerland respectively, active from the 1730s onwards. The Victoria and Albert Museum has an example from the workshops of each of these two famous makers. They are characteristic of English eighteenth-century harpsichords: built to a large scale, with a variety of effects such as the harp and the lute stop, and provided with a mechanism to control the volume. Indeed, Burkat Shudi patented the 'Venetian swell', a series of louvres which opened and closed in an attempt to imitate some of the dynamic effects which were already being achieved on the piano, a new instrument which was to become of great importance in the last quarter of the eighteenth century. As players became more aware of the opportunities offered by the piano, the harpsichord became obsolete and by the early nineteenth century they were no longer made.

The Victoria and Albert Museum has two clavichords in its collection, one by Barthold Fritz (21) and the other by Peter Hicks (22). The instrument has its origins in the medieval monochord, and a sound is produced when a blade, or tangent, touches the string and causes it to vibrate from the point of contact to when it winds round the wrest-pin. Once the tangent is released, the felt placed at the opposite end of the string stifles the sound. This means that the note will ring only so long as the key is pressed down. It is possible to produce a tremolo by varying the pressure on the key. The clavichord, with its soft, dreamy tone, was particularly favoured in Germany and Scandinavia, with C.P.E. Bach being the chief exponent. If the 'Peter Hicks' is English, as the inscription would suggest, it is an object of great rarity, the only signed English clavichord of that period. However, there is reason to doubt the inscription.

There is a small collection of organs, which span 160 years. They are mostly chamber organs, built for private residences and music rooms rather than churches. The sound is produced by blowing wind through pipes, whose length determines the pitch. The air is provided by bellows, which are operated either by the player or by someone specially assigned to the task. The airflow is regulated by trackers, connected to the pipes by means of a pallet with openings at one end, and to the keys by means of a rod attached to a horizontal lever, or back-fall, at the other. The smallest organ in the Victoria and Albert Museum collection is a single manual positive organ (24), probably built by Gottfried Fritzsche for Johann Georg I, Duke of Saxony. This would have been set on a table, with the wind being provided by bellows at the back. The largest organ in the collection was built by John Crang, and this had ten ranks of pipes. It was built for the music room of Fonthill Splendens, the house of Alderman Beckford, to help to develop the talents of his son, William Beckford the Younger. By the mid eighteenth century, it had become fashionable to include a music room in the layout of a new house and to adorn it with a new organ. In the third edition of Chippendale's *The Gentleman and Cabinet maker* (1761), there are some six designs for organ-cases.

The pianoforte was developed at the end of the seventeenth century by Bartolomeo Cristofori, a Florentine harpsichord maker in charge of the musical instrument collection of Ferdinand dei Medici. He called his instrument a 'Gravicembalo col piano e forte'. He devised an 'escapement', whereby the hammer would strike the strings and then, unlike in the clavichord, fall back, both leaving the strings free to vibrate and being ready to strike the strings again when required. In Germany, in the 1730s, Gottfried Silbermann studied Cristofori's invention, made known by an essay by Scipione Maffei, and built his own instrument, earning an enthusiastic response from Frederick the Great. The earliest piano in the Victoria and Albert Museum collection (25) is by Johann Christoff Zumpe, an immigrant from Saxony, who trained under Silbermann in his native country and under Burkat Shudi in London. It was on a piano by Zumpe that Johann Christian Bach gave the first public piano recital in England, in 1768. The instrument is fitted with an 'English action' which does without Cristofori's escapement. However, these compactly designed pianos could be made at an economic price, and then became fashionable not only in England and Europe but also in the Middle East (where, it is said, the legs were shortened so that the player could sit on the floor!). The eighteenth-century pianos in the Victoria and Albert Museum collection are small 'square pianos'; the term came to be used to describe oblong pianos, thus differentiating between them and grand pianos.

The principal centre of piano making on the continent at the turn of the century was Vienna, where makers specialised in a lighter touch, thanks to the development of the 'Viennese action' by Johann Andreas Stein, who earned the praise of Mozart. In the eighteenth century, what was known as 'Turkish music' became fashionable. The use of drums and cymbals in imitation of Janissary bands called for a profusion of pedals to create such effects. This is the case with a forte-piano by Georg Haschka (33) and the

'A Tender Chord' (1907) by
Sir William Quiller Orchardson R.A.
(1832-1910), depicting the grand piano
by Georg Haschka, Vienna, c. 1815-20
(33). The instrument was presented
to the Museum by the painter.
Reproduced by courtesy of Courtauld
Institute of Art.

Van der Does 'Giraffe piano' (*colour plate* VIII), a Dutch imitation of a Viennese upright grand, which date respectively from about 1815 and 1820.

In the nineteenth century, the piano underwent alterations which transformed it into a modern instrument. By the mid-century, the keyboard compass had been extended from the five octaves to which Mozart, Haydn and Beethoven had been accustomed to seven and a half octaves. Henri Pape, who was employed in the workshop of Ignace Pleyel, perhaps the greatest piano maker of the first half of that century, patented the felt hammer. The brittle deer-skin hammer was replaced by this more durable material, which could stand up to the tougher demands of modern playing techniques. Perhaps the most important innovation was the introduction of the metal frame to counteract the strain imposed by the more heavily gauged strings. Such an idea would have been as treasonable to the eighteenth-century player as, say, the introduction of a metal frame to the body of a violin. This was pioneered in America, where extremes of climate prompted an Englishman, Isaac Hawkins, to make an upright piano with a large amount of metal in the frame. In 1825, Alpheus Babcock of Boston cast the whole frame of a square piano as one piece of iron. As the century progressed, metal was used more often in European and American pianos, with construction being brought to perfection by Henry Steinway and his son Theodore, a trained acoustician and physicist. They achieved their results by giving their pianos a complete cast-iron frame and cross-stringing, as opposed to parallel stringing. The principle whereby the treble strings were set perpendicularly and the bass strings cross at a diagonal, thus being allowed more length than with parallel stringing, had been tried in the eighteenth century and became normal for upright pianos after about 1828, mainly to improve the tone of the bass. The Steinways used cross-stringing and adjusted both the spaces between the strings and the position of the bridge so that the strings could vibrate most effectively.

During the same period, the modern upright piano was developed, in response to increasing demands for a more powerful instrument than the square piano and for one that would take up less room than a grand. Among the middle classes pianos were being acquired in ever-increasing numbers, as a status symbol and as the chief source of family entertainment. The idea of an upright keyboard instrument was not new; the clavicytherium, the upright version, had been in existence almost as long as the harpsichord. In 1800, both Isaac Hawkins in Philadelphia and Mathias Müller in Vienna, quite independently from one another, hit upon the idea of upending a grand piano, resting the tail at the bottom and placing the wrest-pins at the top. In 1807, William Southwell built upended pianos on a larger scale – they were known as cabinet pianos. In 1811, Robert Wornum produced a small upright piano, called a cottage piano, which was later to undergo such alterations as cross-stringing and the tape-check action, a device whereby a tape attached to a hammer-butt speeds the return of the hammer to its original position, so that it does not simply rely on gravity; this device permitted more rapid playing.

The two most impressive nineteenth-century grands in the Victoria and Albert Museum collection are the one made by John Broadwood and Sons (39 and 40), with a case made and decorated by William Morris & Co., and Henry Cole's piano (38). In the latter, we see Wornum's inventiveness at work: a downward-striking hammer is used so as to avoid unseating the strings, a problem which occurred with the more orthodox up-striking hammers. More interesting, if only for their decorative uses, are the massive 'Gothic' pianos by Collard and Collard, a firm which carried on from a company set up by Muzio Clementi, the virtuoso and composer. These instruments are lavishly decorated, one being designed by Charles Bevan (36), who was responsible for other furniture in this style from 1865 to 1871. The Burne-Jones piano (35) was, from a musicological point of view, a modest instrument; its interest lies in the fact that it is decorated with one of his paintings, 'Le Chant d'Amour'.

An inevitable result of the Industrial Revolution was that mass-production was increasingly used in the building of pianos. Thus, as the nineteenth century progressed pianos for the most part took on a machine-made appearance, lacking the meticulously inlaid and painted decoration of the early keyboard instruments or the classical simplicity of those of the seventeenth century. However, there was a revival of interest in the decoration of piano cases at the end of the century, one of the most famous examples being the Baillie Scott 'Manxman' (41), whose keyboard far from protruding is concealed behind shutters. The Victoria and Albert Museum is fortunate in having some of the most beautifully decorated pianos of the nineteenth century, where standards of design remained high.

The Colour Plates

1 **Virginal**
Northern European, *c.* 1600
Museum No. 420-1872

The instrument is richly decorated
with coloured glass and the lid
contains scenes from Ovid's
Metamorphoses. This was probably
always more of a showpiece than a
serious instrument. It is possibly the
'musical instrument made all of
glass, except the strings', seen by
Paul Heutzner at Hampton Court in
1598. The keyboard compass
comprises forty-five notes, C/E – c^3.

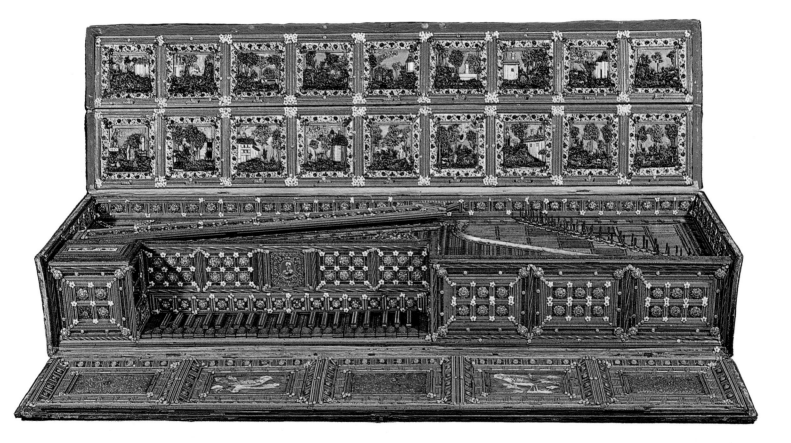

11 **Spinet**
('Queen Elizabeth's Virginals')
probably Venetian, *c.* 1570
Museum No. 19-1887

The instrument is richly decorated
with moresques in red and blue
glazes on a gilded ground. On the
far right panel is the badge used by
Anne Boleyn and Queen Elizabeth I,
and on the far left the Royal arms of
the Tudor monarchs. The present
keyboard compass comprises fifty
notes, GG/BB – c³.

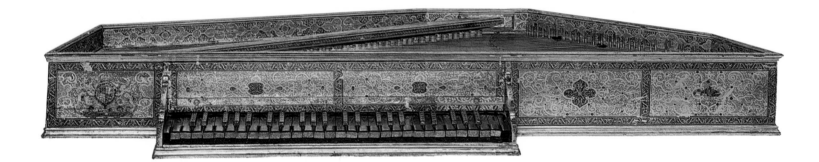

III Virginal
Flemish, 1568
Museum No. 447-1896

The instrument was made for
William, Duke of Cleves (1516-92).
Its case is of walnut, decorated with
carved musical trophies. On the
inside of the lid, strapwork surrounds
a medallion of Orpheus and the wild
beasts. The original keyboard
compass is believed to have
comprised forty-five notes, C/E – c³.

IV **Spinet**
Annibale dei Rossi, Milan, 1577
Museum No. 809-1869

The instrument is richly decorated
with semi-precious stones, set on a
ground of ebony and ivory. It is
almost certainly the instrument 'of
uncommon beauty and excellence,
with the keys all of precious stones,
and with their most elegant
ornaments', described in Merigi's
La Nobilità di Milano (1595) as having
belonged to the scholar Carlo
Trivulzio. The keyboard compass
comprises fifty notes, C/E – f³.

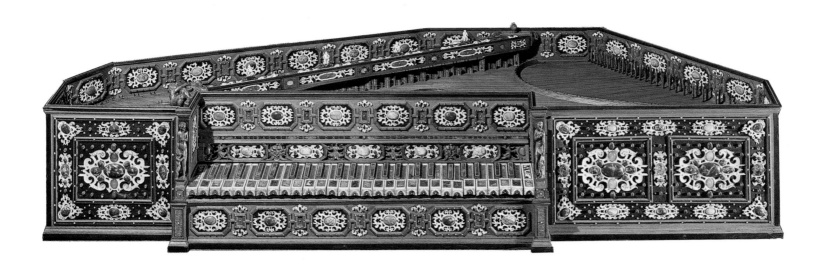

v Octave spinet
Italian, *c.* 1600
Museum No. 218-1870

The small instrument is made of
cypress wood and can be moved
from its case. The inside of the lid is
decorated with the story of Arion
and the dolphin, and that of the
keyboard cover with groups of
dancing maenads and music-making
putti. The keyboard compass
comprises forty-five notes, C/E – c³.

VI **Harpsichord**
Jean-Antoine Vaudry, Paris, 1681
Museum No. W12-1974

This exceptionally important instrument of the seventeenth century formed part of a claviorganum. The inside of the lid is decorated with chinoiserie figures and the sound-board with various flowers in gouache. The keyboard compass comprises fifty notes, GG/BB short octave – c³. There are three sets of strings and a coupler for both manuals. Jean-Antoine Vaudry seems to have supplied instruments to the French court of Louis XIV.

VII **Harpsichord**
Pascal Taskin, Paris, 1786
Museum No. 1121-1869

The instrument is the only known
example of a harpsichord with a
miniature keyboard compass made
by a harpsichord builder of the first
rank. The case and the inside of the
lid are decorated with japanned
chinoiserie figures in fantastic
landscapes. The keyboard is made
specially narrow either for a child's
or an exceptionally small adult's
hands. Its compass comprises
sixty-two notes, EE – f³.

VIII **Upright piano**
Van der Does, Amsterdam, *c.* 1820
Museum No. 461-1907

The instrument reflects the popularity of Viennese pianos on the continent. One variant, such as this, was upright and owing to its curious shape came to be called the 'Giraffe piano'. The keyboard compass comprises seventy-three notes, FF – f⁴.

The instrument was presented to the Museum by Sir William Quiller Orchardson, R.A., who depicted it in two of his paintings, 'Music when soft voices die' (1893) and 'The Lyric' (1904).

The Plates

1 **Harpsichord**
Jerome of Bologna, Rome, 1521
Museum No. 226-1879

This is one of the earliest dated
harpsichords to survive. The
instrument is of cypress, and the
leather outer case, with gilt tooling,
is seventeenth-century. The present
keyboard compass is forty-seven
notes, C – d³, with a C/E short octave.
The original compass comprised
probably fifty notes, C/E – f³.

2 Spinet
Italian, mid sixteenth century
Museum No. 490-1899

The instrument is of cypress wood, decorated on the inside with scroll work of silver gilt gesso on a blue ground. The present keyboard compass comprises forty-nine notes, F – f³ chromatic. The sharps are ebony and the naturals are boxwood covered. It still has its outer case (not shown here) to protect it when not in use, as when travelling.

3 Spinet

Annibale dei Rossi, Milan, 1555
Museum No. 156-1869

The instrument is of cypress wood,
with the inner faces being finely
carved. It was once part of a
claviorgan, a combination of spinet
or harpsichord and organ. The
keyboard comprises fifty notes,
C/E – f³, with a bass short octave.

4 Spinet

Marco Iadra, Italian, 1568
Museum No. 155-1869

The instrument is decorated with
Mannerist arabesques and fitted with
ebony mouldings. The keyboard
compass comprises fifty notes, C/E
short octave – f³, with the ivory keys
being made of fine Gothic arcading.

5 Harpsichord

Giovanni Antonio Baffo, Venice, 1574
Museum No. 6007-1859

The inside of the lid derives its decoration from the painted ceilings of contemporary Venetian palaces. The outer case shown here is decorated with the original gilt moresques. The keyboard compass comprises fifty notes, GG/BB – c³, having been altered some sixty years after the instrument was built. The end was truncated, probably in the second half of the eighteenth century.

6 Claviorgan
Lodewyk Theewes, London, 1579
Museum No. 125-1890

This combination of harpsichord and organ is the sole extant English keyboard instrument of the sixteenth century, and only the outer case and fragments of the workings survive. The remaining structure is of oak decorated with panels of painted strapwork and articulated with ionic pilasters. The coats of arms are those of the Roper family.
The instrument was given by Mrs Luard-Selby in 1890.

7 Claviorgan
Lodewyk Theewes
Detail of (6): the inside of the lid

This is a very fine and rare example
of English Elizabethan decorative
painting. Strapwork enframes a
cartouche in which Orpheus is
depicted playing to the wild beasts.
There are Italianate-like swags of
fruit and Etruscan sphynxes.

8 Octave spinet
Anonymous, German, *c.* 1625-50
Museum No. 4265-1857

The instrument is of ebony, decorated
with silver, an example of the
cabinets d'Allemagne, made by the
silversmiths of Augsburg, as
expensive and highly prized presents.
A secret drawer is concealed in the
plinth of the instrument. The lid
contains a box whose lid forms a
sloping writing desk. The keyboard
compass comprises thirty-eight notes,
$G - g^2$, a^2.

9 **Harpsichord**
Andreas Ruckers the Elder,
Antwerp, 1631
Museum No. 1079-1868.

The instrument was completely
rebuilt and decorated in the second
half of the eighteenth century, when
the present keyboards were inserted.

Their compasses are fifty-eight notes,
GG, AA – f³. The instrument has
three sets of strings controlled by
three stop-knobs of which two are
visible on the left.
The instrument was presented by
John Broadwood & Sons in 1868.

10 **Harpsichord**
Ioannes Ruckers, Antwerp, 1639
Museum No. 1739-1869

The instrument was owned by
George III until 1766. The keyboard
and stand were destroyed in a fire
at the Kirckman piano factory in
1853. The decoration is from the
second half of the eighteenth
century.
The instrument was given by Messrs
Kirckman & Sons in 1869.

11 **Virginal**
Thomas White, London, 1642
Museum No. W11-1933

The case is decorated with gilt and
embossed paper. Pastoral scenes are
painted on the inside of the lid. The
naturals are boxwood and the
sharps stained hardwood. The
keyboard compass comprises forty-
nine notes, C – c³ chromatic.
The instrument was given by Mrs
Ada Deacon in 1933.

◄ 12 **Virginal**
John Loosemore, Exeter, 1655
Museum No. 813-1873

The inside of the instrument is decorated with gilt embossed paper, the characteristic English form based on Flemish models. On the lid and drop front are depicted a variety of animals (including a turkey), pastoral scenes and the story of Adam and Eve. The keyboard compass comprises fifty-one notes, C – d³ chromatic.

13 **Spinet**
John Player, London, last quarter of the seventeenth century
Museum No. 466-1882

The case is of oak and the stand is of turned oak, apparently original. In the second half of the seventeenth century, rectangular virginals became obsolete and wing-shaped spinets such as this became fashionable. The keyboard compass comprises fifty-one notes, GG – c³, with a broken octave and split C-sharp and D-sharp keys.

14 Harpsichord
Thomas Hitchcock, London, *c.* 1725
Museum No. 126-1890

The case of the instrument is of
walnut with a double curve to the
bent-side. The stand is of beech,
stained to match the case. There are
four sets of strings, but the stop
knobs are missing. The keyboard
compass comprises sixty-one notes,
GG – g³, chromatic, and the sharps
are skunk-tailed (i.e. ebony with an
ivory slip).

15 Harpsichord
('The Ham House Ruckers'),
English, *c.* 1730
Museum No. HH109-1948

The construction of this instrument reveals it to be a fine English harpsichord of *c.* 1730 but it is dated 1634 and bears the name of Ioannes Ruckers, the famous Antwerp maker of the seventeenth century. The case is also decorated in the Ruckers manner. It was meant to look like one and was believed to be such until the 1960s. Ruckers instruments were much prized in the eighteenth century and the keyboards were often enlarged so as to adapt old instruments to the requirements of modern music.

16 **Spinet**
John Crang, London, 1758
Museum No. W16-1947

The case is veneered with panels of
burr walnut and crossbanded
unfigured walnut and decorated
with boxwood and ebony stringing.
The nameboard is adorned with a
fine trophy of musical instruments,
executed in marquetry. The keyboard
has a compass of sixty-one notes,
GG – g^3 chromatic, and the keys
are balanced with lead weights.
The instrument was bequeathed by
Miss C. A. R. Adams in 1947.

17 Spinet
Baker Harris, London, 1770
Museum No. W14-1943

The case and lid of the instrument
are of mahogany. The case is
decorated with cross-banding and
stringing of sycamore and ebony.
The central panel, on which the
inscription is placed, is of sycamore.
The keyboard compass comprises
sixty notes, FF, GG – f³ chromatic.
The instrument was given by Charles
Hey Laycock in 1943.

18 **Spinet**
Joseph Mahoon, London, 1771
Museum No. 383-1907

The case of the instrument is
mahogany, cross-banded with
sycamore stringing. Panels of walnut
are placed above the keyboard.
The fronts of the naturals are
arcaded. The keyboard compass
comprises sixty-one notes, GG – g³
chromatic.

19 Harpsichord
Jacob and Abraham Kirckman,
London, 1776
Museum No. w43-1927

The instrument is characteristic
of late eighteenth-century English
harpsichords, with a machine stop
and nag's head swell, and a flap inside
the lid, which opened and closed to
control the volume. The case is
veneered with mahogany inlaid with
sycamore stringing. There are three
sets of strings, and the keyboard
compass comprises sixty notes,
FF – f³ chromatic, lacking FF sharp.
The instrument was given by Mr
F. S. Dayman in 1927.

20 Harpsichord

Shudi and Broadwood, London, 1782
Museum No. W13-1943

The instrument is characteristic of
large English harpsichords at the end
of the eighteenth century, when the
harpsichord was, as it were, fighting
a rearguard action against the
pianoforte which was fast gaining
in popularity. The case and lid are
veneered with mahogany and
cross-banded with satinwood.

Beneath the lid lies the 'Venetian
swell', a set of twelve louvres which
open and close to vary the volume.
They are controlled by the right
pedal. The player has a choice
between hand-stops or the machine
stop which is controlled from the
left pedal. The keyboard compass
comprises sixty-six notes, CC – f³
chromatic.
The instrument was given by Charles
Hey Laycock in 1943.

21 Clavichord
Barthold Fritz, Brunswick, 1751
Museum No. 339-1882

The instrument is a standard large German harpsichord. It is decorated with a blue monochrome hunting scene, something very rare with German instruments. The keyboard compass comprises sixty-five notes, FF – a³ chromatic.

22 Clavichord
'Peter Hicks', late eighteenth century
Museum No. w7-1917

The case is mahogany. The difference in workmanship between the case and soundboard suggests that an amateur restoration was made. The inscription may have been added but the instrument is unique in being of mahogany although built on German lines. The keyboard compass comprises fifty-one notes, C – d³, and the tangents are brass.

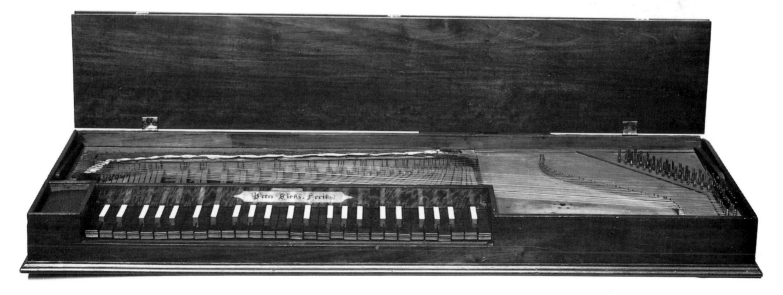

23 Cabinet organ
South German, early seventeenth century
Museum No. 216-1879

The upper part of the cabinet dates from the late sixteenth century, being decorated in marquetry on a pine carcase. The lower part, which contains the playing mechanism, was built in the early seventeenth century and painted with imitation marquetry to match the upper part. The bellows are worked by a pedal by the front right-hand leg. The keyboard, whose design is derived from Praetorius (1619), has a compass of forty-one notes, E – g^2, a^2.

24 Positive organ
German, *c.* 1627
Museum No. 2-1867

This small organ would have been set on a table, with one person playing and another working the bellows at the back. The story of Abraham is depicted on the shutters and a medallion portrait of Duke Johann Georg of Saxony is included in the pipe shade. The top of the instrument is decorated with Northern Renaissance strapwork. The keyboard compass comprises forty-one notes, $C/E - g^2$, a^2, and the pipes are made of layered paper.

48

25 Square piano
Johann Christoff Zumpe,
London, 1767
Museum No. w27-1928

This is one of the very earliest
English pianos to survive. The case
is made of mahogany with stringing
of boxwood or holly. The keyboard
compass comprises apparently fifty-
nine notes, GG – f³, but GG sharp
is dummy. The instrument is fitted
with the English single action. On a
piano such as this, Johann Christian
Bach gave the first public piano
recital in England.

26 Square piano

Johannes Pohlmann, London, 1773
Museum No. OPH158-1949

The instrument forms part of the furnishings of Osterley Park House and would have been an expensive novelty when acquired by Robert Childe or his wife, when the first of his Adams rooms had just been completed. The case and stand are mahogany. The keyboard has a compass of sixty-one notes, FF – f³, and the dampers and buff-stop are controlled by the brass levers on the left. The instrument is fitted with Zumpe's single English action.

27, 28 Square piano
Christopher Ganer, London, *c.* 1780
Museum No. w75-1975

The case is veneered in mahogany with a satinwood and marquetry decoration. The medallions at the heads of the legs are of gilt. The instrument is fitted with the English single action.

The keyboard compass comprises sixty-one notes, FF – f³ chromatic. The fronts of the naturals are moulded stained wood. The nameboard is decorated with a neo-classical ribbon and swag motif. The piano was given by Miss F. M. Harris in 1975.

29 Square piano
Longman & Broderip,
London, *c.* 1795
Museum No. w33-1964

The case is of mahogany and the
nameboard of satinwood, decorated
with painted swags at either end of
the plaque and with pierced patterns
at both ends. The instrument has an
English single action with crank
dampers and the keyboard has a
compass of sixty-eight notes, FF – c^4
chromatic.
The piano was given by Mr Guy
Jonson in 1969.

30 Square piano
John Broadwood & Son
London, 1801
Museum No. hh433-1948

The piano is part of the furnishings
of Ham House. It is concealed in a
sofa table, disguised as a drawer,
and is pulled out for playing. The
table is of veneered mahogany with
stringing of ebony and boxwood,
and the stand is an ornate variation
of a trestle design. The keyboard
compass comprises sixty-one notes,
FF – f^3, and the instrument is bichord
strung throughout and fitted with
the English single action.

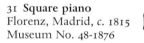

31 Square piano
Florenz, Madrid, *c.* 1815
Museum No. 48-1876

The instrument, of rosewood and
mahogany, is decorated with
medallions which were made to
resemble Wedgwood jasperware.
It was probably inspired by a
Broadwood piano presented to
Queen Maria Luisa de Parma of
Spain by Manuel Godoy, the then
prime minister. The keyboard
compass comprises sixty-eight notes,
FF – c⁴, the seven additional notes
being produced by hammers through
a slot at the edge of the soundboard.

32 Pianino
Chappell & Co., London, *c.* 1815
Museum No. w2-1919

The instrument was possibly used
to provide the pitch for choral
groups. The sound is produced by
hammers striking glass rods. The
case is veneered in mahogany and
the nameboard in satinwood. The
keyboard compass comprises thirty-
one notes, c – c³.
The instrument was given by
Mr Edmund Davis in 1919.

33 Grand piano
Georg Haschka, Vienna, *c*. 1815-20
Museum No. 460-1907

The piano is decorated in a
flamboyant if somewhat debased
Empire style. On the inside of the
lid is depicted the story of Samson
and the lion. The keyboard has a
compass of seventy-three notes,
FF – f⁴, and is fitted with the
Viennese action. Eight pedals control
a number of effects, such as bassoon,
triangle and drum.
The instrument was presented by
Sir William Quiller Orchardson,
R.A., who depicted it in 'A Tender
Chord' in 1907.

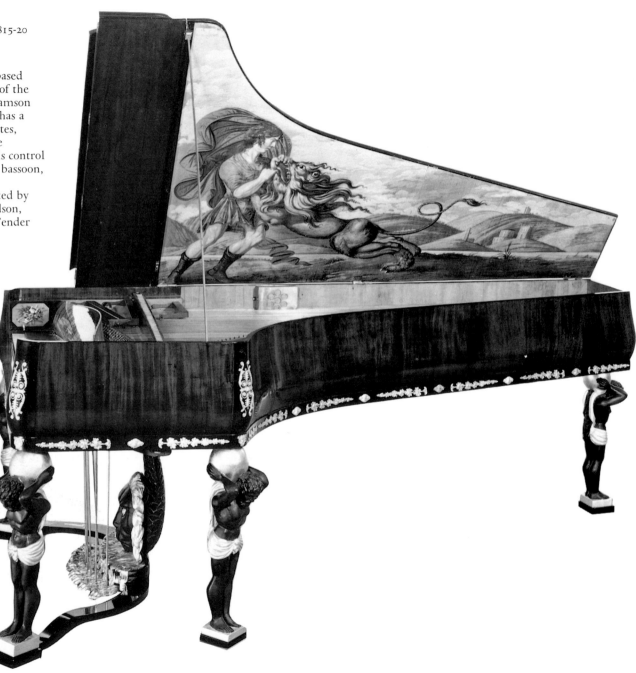

34 Upright piano (Euphonicon)
English, *c.* 1840
Museum No. 342-1874

This unorthodox instrument,
invented by Dr John Steward of
Wolverhampton in 1840, is built
against a harp-shaped metal frame,
and uses 'f'-holed sound boxes rather
than a soundboard. The case is of
rosewood and the boxes have spruce
fronts and sycamore backs and sides.
The pedals are used to raise dampers
and shift the action to *una corda*.
The keyboard compass comprises
eight notes, CC – g^4.

35 Upright piano
F. Priestly, London, *c.* 1860
Museum No. w43-1926

The case of this very ordinary
upright piano was painted and
lacquered by Sir Edward Burne-
Jones, with scenes from 'Le Chant
d'Amour'. The keyboard compass
comprises eighty-two notes, CC – a⁴.
The instrument was given by
Mrs J. W. Mackail in 1926.

36 Upright piano
Collard and Collard, *c.* 1865
Museum No. w6-1968

The case of the instrument is veneered with satinwood and richly inlaid. It is probably designed by Charles Bevan, who made similar furniture in a reformed Gothic style. The keyboard has a compass of eighty-five notes, AAA – a^4, and the piano is fitted with a tape-check sticker upright action with overdampers.

37 Upright piano
Collard and Collard, London, 1855-75
Museum No. W20-1974

The instrument is decorated in a neo-Gothic style, reflecting contemporary German influence. The keyboard compass comprises eighty-five notes, AAA – a^4, and the action is of a simple sticker type, without tapes.

38 Grand piano
Robert Wornum & Sons,
London, *c.* 1870
Museum No. W11-1913

This piano belonged to Sir Henry
Cole, the Museum's first director.
The case is painted with designs by
John Gamble. The piano is fitted

with Robert Wornum's downward
striking action, and its keyboard
compass comprises eighty-five notes,
AAA – a⁴.
The instrument was given by Mr
Alan Cole, one of Sir Henry's sons.

39, 40 Grand piano
John Broadwood & Sons,
London, 1883
Museum No. w23-1927

The case of the instrument is
decorated with silver gilt and gesso
on a green ground. The design was
taken from a sketch by Sir Edward
Burne-Jones and developed in detail
by Kate Faulkner of William Morris
& Co. The keyboard compass
comprises eighty-five notes,
AAA – a⁴, with an English check-
action and underdampers to b².
The instrument was given by
Mrs A. C. Ionides.

41 Upright piano
John Broadwood & Son,
London, *c*. 1903
Museum No. W15-1976

The instrument is the 'Manxman' model designed by M. H. Baillie-Scott and perhaps the first example where the keyboard is enclosed in a case. The outside of the doors is decorated with floral motifs in the style of the Arts and Crafts movement and the inside of the lid with a striking checker-board pattern. The keyboard compass comprises eight-five notes, AAA – a^4, and the instrument is fitted with the standard tape-check action.

42 Upright piano ▶
Roemhildt, Weimar, 1906
Museum No. Circ. 476-1967

The case of the instrument was designed by Henry van de Velde (1863-1957), a prominent member of the Art Nouveau (*Jugendstil*) movement. The inscription is in that style. The keyboard compass comprises eighty-five notes, AAA – a^4, and the action is tape-checked.